BEYOND THE
HALF-LIGHT

SWETHA PV

BookLeaf
Publishing

India | USA | UK

Made with ❤ on the BookLeaf Publishing Platform
www.bookleafpub.in
www.bookleafpub.com

Dedication

For my family, my forever blessing

Preface

Beyond the Half-Light is a book born where love softens the world and longing carves out its own space. Within these pages live twenty poems- warm with romance and shadowed by ache, written in the in-between spaces we rarely name aloud - HALF LIGHT! It is a place where clarity begins to form but mystery still lingers.

My first book 'Between', was a home for my beginnings. This second book arrives as the bridge beyond that space. I write from the Half-Light, where hope and hurt become tangents. It is a space of becoming, where wounds haven't healed fully yet hope has already begun to bloom. Here, love is a promise to remain soft in a world that bruises, and anxiety is a pulse and a proof of feeling deeply and never a flaw.

If these words find you in your own Half-Light, may they hold you gently. May they remind you that 'to feel deeply is to live truly'.

Thank you for stepping into this Half-Light with me. Let us travel a little beyond it

Acknowledgements

With gratitude that lives deeper than words!

To the ones who watered my dreams,
gathered my broken pieces without complaint
and loved me into becoming...
You are the blessing I return to, again and again...
And..
To my Publisher, for giving these pages a home in this world...

1. Hearth & Heart

Oh...
to fall into you, my leaf
as a tiny droplet of mist...
to build a home so serene
that would drive away my woes...
to knead doughs so thick
only to render it thin and fine...
to knit yellow crochets
beside the flickering fireplace...
to write loads of poetry
only for you to recite...
to pluck juicy lemons
from among the sour bunches...
to read verses of Odyssey
for the long path yet to travel...
to carry heavy pumpkins
from the Eden garden together...
to be the calm water lily
for the mighty moon that you are...

2. Dust and Grime

Dust and grime
embracing tiny nails
Walking barefoot,
day and night...

Dust and grime
oozing through the gorge
adorning freckles
and lazy prints...

Dust and grime
in all its sparkle
shining bright over
the familiar labyrinth...

Dust and grime
sharp yet smooth,
sculpting grace
from the foot of might...

Dust and grime
so wonderfully prime,
making me adore
the swiftness of time...

3. The Last Metro

A cursory glance,
but a significant stare
Out there I strolled,
the path not unknown...

Among the crowd,
amidst the chaos
a pair of doe eyes
was the only sight...

Opened doors, cleared signals,
Nothing on earth
stopped us from the
reverie, so serene...

Knitting the eyelashes
of that fantasy in a crochet,
Together we smiled
staring at the last metro...

4. A shelter that breathes...

Strolling for hours,
searching for a shelter
vocals dried up; and
even the wind pipe...

A squinted glance
Ah yes...! Found a tree
A tress less immaculate
for the leaves to live on

The branches turned a deaf ear;
no birds to build a nest
It seems, even the dry brown leaves
were embarrassed to show up...

I stared at the tree
It stared back at me...
It was hard to tell apart
whose existence was am eroteme !

5. Where promises sleep...

Could someone lend me an abode?
An abode of unfinished hopes,
uncherished dreams
and unending promises..
.

Like the sky that
cradles birds of paradise...
Like the sea that
embraces schools of fish...
Like the soil that
hugs insects tight...

I asked for gentleness...
To breathe between storms...

Alas! The abode with
the promising promises
wrapped me close
only to tighten its grip...

Like the flame that invites
and devours all the same...
Like the serpent whose
warmth is just a waiting game...

Like the lightning that
is sudden, and never merciful.....

Yes! They lent me an abode!
And I lay in it,
Folded in silence,
never to wake up again...

6. Yellow

A colour so bright, yet so light
Erasing the sorrows, of all tomorrows

In the warmth of wilted pages,
in the fields of merry mustards
Yellow arrives raw, carrying its honeyed glow...

A colour so bold, but never loud
Humming the tune of mild uncertainty

Through wild sunflower fields
Through marigold blossoms
Yellow stays, while all others fade...

7. Shadow's Grin

Rain dissolved
clouds stilled

Shutters locked
Footsteps unclear

Echoes sealed
Void and Vile

An eerie howl
cuts the dark

A shadow leans
but never speaks

A lopsided grin
With no mouth

A mirrored soul
is watching you

8. Becoming

And like the fish
let me swim through
the darkest hours
and waves of life!

And like the ocean
let me thrive through
the future, hugging all
the inmates tight!

And like the firefly
let me flicker bright across
the honeyed hills of
hope and happiness!

And like the starfish
let me retreat, unseen
from the masked enemies
into the sea of hues!

And like the caterpillar
let me emerge out in
silence to become the
prettiest living creature!

And like the water
let me flow through it all;
above the test of time,
forever finding my way!

9. If this dream is where you belong...

The morning sun bows down to you
The cynosure of every gaze, my love...
What is this loop of love I've got into?
Is this a dream already conquered?
The stars are hiding behind the veils
Only for your eyes to shine bright
Should I rise and leave this dream behind?
Or ask sleep to embrace me again?
The moon throws that smile on to you
for the lilies to have a glance
Oh let me dive into deep sleep,
a sleep where love is real

.

10. Rust and Reverie

A crippling anxiety
unending fatigue
creepy noises seeping through,
concrete walls of brick
Ah! a swish of satin cloth
caught hold of flashbacks...
Jasmine wound hair buns...
Aroma of freshly brewed coffee...
Tuneless humming from the courtyard...
Peek-a-boos from doors behind...
Why do we borrow moments from the past?
Curling up under the comfort
of the days bygone,
slipping into reminiscence...
Moments, memories
and nostalgia;
Only a curve of rainbow
before the downpour...

11. Hope

Walking amidst purpled plums
and poking tangy peaches
Watering my wistful mind
with the misty droplets of yore
I dream of subtle refrains
where my love will reside
soft and calm, drenched
in the rain of passion...
Wandering through remote browns,
emerald greens and mustard yellows
beside slivers of sunlight, my pal,
I search for hums and tunes of
long forgotten shades
and a bridge of colours so bright
Hoping love would come
knocking at my door again...

12. Swing of Time

The tassels of the past
are here to stay
hanging like the bob
of a pendulum;
moving to and fro
dictating the flow of time
the silent sway
the uniform pulse
untouched by time
is here to stay;
measuring the depth of
the days bygone;
bittersweet yet redemptive
they are here to stay...
Each arc a reminder,
each swing an unbroken echo,
The metal neither fades, nor sleeps
enduring the test of time,
a quiet testament
a subtle defiance
they are here to stay...

13. A Bitter Refrain...

Fortitude rose where gratitude knelt
Strength melted into a prayer, unspoken
She was sunlit, but now weary
A tide of warmth, now a still wave
What else could this realm
of time shower upon her?
Time silenced her soul
or was it fate that made her mercurial?
Mirth has now turned plaintive
as she stood staring at the hallowed ground

There shall never be a never-never land
'Win laurels' echoed the old sound
Her loss- would slip down her throat
like a hot lump of ash,
only to leave a hollow,
where dreams used to bloom...

14. Dawn

A fleeting glance on the ground
I fumbled upon the stones
He led me up the hill
to the highest slope
where winds echoed
where earth met the sky
where hearts gasped
I worked up the nerve
to keep up the word
Down I jumped,
High I flew,
Chasing horizons
Destinations unknown
It's all a continuum
We are taking the right turns,
weaving the best of our stories...

15. The Detour

A mundane Monday it was
packed with things quotidian
A gust of cool gale
like glitter on the galaxy
pierced the atrium
of my once broken heart...

What was this pang
that healed me at length
with the glance of the
lady in moist maroon?
Was she the missing puzzle
to the labyrinth my heart is...?

Days passed, nights moved
We watered the camaraderie
with convos from deep within,
Songs heard, food shared
Exchanged bedsheets
had stories to tell...

Thursday arrived unfairly
for us to walk away
The man in the uniform

distanced her luggage from mine
Shared laughter, uncherished dreams
paved the way for tears...

Then came the fictitious Friday
with a rain so random
Families met with words so fruitful
'that marriage is nothing, but
the union of hearts, and
then our eyes met...

Those eyes were familiar
with the twinkle from our future
It wasn't a pang
but a fervour so obvious
Yes, she was the missing puzzle
to the labyrinth my heart is...

16. The Weight of Now

They said,
'Carve out a niche',
Well, it runs in your blood,
unshaken!'
But was that right?
Carving my way out
through the thorny walkway
only to be left with
quiet disappointment
They said,
'live in the present'
Well, that's the way to live
holding today, in the pulse of
the present...
But is that all?
Letting my spirit chase
the fleeting moments;
breathing in the present
only to collapse in the end...

17. Second Bloom

Oh love,
let the darkest days of your life
turn into the kohl lining your eyes
let the blood oozing out of your soul
adorn your rosy rosy lips
let the tears rolling down your cheeks
brighten your face with its shimmer
let the tiny shattered pieces of your heart
build an armour for the lady that you are...

18. Stillness

A flooding of nerve ends, blue and thin
ignited by the swing, soft and quiet
moving languorously
drifting; easy and eerie...
fear and a gentle ache
despair disdain and a veiled disgust
wandering wide, unbound and unseen
echoing tremors of the heart's unrest...
The lingering trace of blood
oozing out of the veins,
ache and a pang
weighing the eyelids down...
A sour thought, inside my mind's room
is getting bruised in quiet ink
but the words fell asleep
in the stillness of what was never said...

19. Seams of Love

As day folds into the arms of twilight
and sun-blessed tides turn moon-kissed;
I surrender to this warm thread of night
to weave a new dawn of gentle hue...

Let our yarns merge and find each other,
in the tranquil stitching of peace;
to spin a shade unknown to the world,
wrapped in the essence of lulled dreams...

Under the enchanted glow of stars a zillion,
Hand-in-hand shall we drape desires of the half moon,
in colours so celestial and reverent
only to shine bright in the darkest of nights...

Gathering the moon-pulled wave of memories
Together with the light of my life, my love,
Here I lie, nestled in your waiting
to sink into the softest slumber...

20. Endless Verse

Your infectious smile is nothing
but a lyric of moonlit words
adorning my darkest nights

Oh, don't fade away my love,
for your sunless cheeks
make my verses barren

The velvet syllables of your gaze
is but a love drenched sonnet,
an art so whole, a prayer to my ears

The metaphor of your being
is nothing but a spell so holy,
a sacred syntax of love

Your eyes hold infinite galaxies,
beautiful beyond reason
a dreamy prose of magic and might

Oh let me bloom allegorically in love,
only to read the poem that you are,
Oh beloved, in you, I begin again...